John F. Kennedy's Inaugural Address

Written by Julia Hargrove

Illustrated by Bron Smith

Teaching & Learning Company

1204 Buchanan St., P.O. Box 10
Carthage, IL 62321-0010

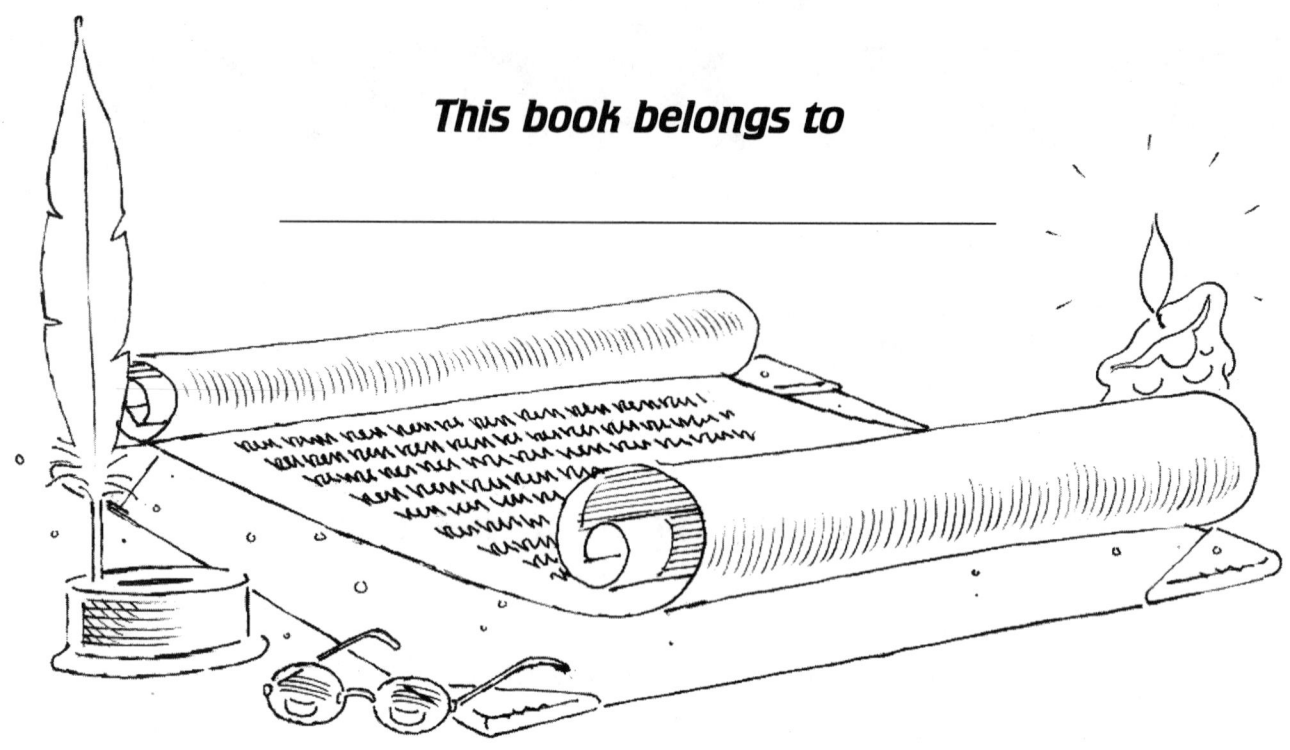

This book belongs to

_____

Cover photo obtained from the Photoduplication Service of the Library of Congress.

Copyright © 2000, Teaching & Learning Company

ISBN No. 1-57310-222-9

Printing No. 987654321

Teaching & Learning Company
1204 Buchanan St., P.O. Box 10
Carthage, IL 62321-0010

The purchase of this book entitles teachers to make copies for use in their individual classrooms only. This book, or any part of it, may not be reproduced in any form for any other purposes without prior written permission from the Teaching & Learning Company. It is strictly prohibited to reproduce any part of this book for an entire school or school district, or for commercial resale. The above permission is exclusive of the cover art, which may not be reproduced.

All rights reserved. Printed in the United States of America.

Table of Contents

John F. Kennedy's Inaugural Address 5
Building a Time Line 11
Cuba and the Cold War Time Line 12
Berlin and the Cold War Time Line 13
Berlin and the Cold War Wring Exercise–Outlining 14
Berlin and the Cold War Writing Exercise–Writing Paragraph 15
Biography of John F. Kennedy 16
President Kennedy and the Cold War–Map Exercise 18
Map of Western Hemisphere 19
Map of Europe 20
Map of Asia 21
Latin America and the Alliance for Progress 22
President Kennedy and the United Nations 24
Multiple Intelligence Activities 26
Internet Research Ideas 29
Answer Key 32

Dear Teacher or Parent,

This book is one in a series by the Teaching & Learning Company which examines famous documents in United States history.

The transition from President Eisenhower to President Kennedy was seen as a crucial change for several reasons. Eisenhower was one of the oldest Presidents, while Kennedy was the youngest person elected to the office. Eisenhower had a heart attack and a mild stroke while in office; Kennedy appeared young, athletic and healthy. Eisenhower was seen by many to be a do-nothing President; Kennedy was vigorous and full of new ideas. Eisenhower had been embarrassed and discredited internationally by the U-2 spy plane scandal.

Kennedy's presidency would give the U.S. a new start with a strong, forceful international policy. As Kennedy put it so eloquently in his inaugural address, ". . . the torch has been passed to a new generation of Americans . . . ," and to many, he embodied new optimism and hope.

Kennedy did accomplish many good things in his nearly three years in office. But because of his assassination, the U.S. can only wonder what he might have accomplished had he lived longer and continued to work towards fulfilling the ideals in his inaugural speech. Was the civil rights legislation passed under Johnson only possible because of Kennedy's death, or could Kennedy have achieved as much or more in his own right? Would Kennedy have taken the course of removing U.S. troops from Vietnam and spared the U.S. that agony, or would he have increased troop strength in Southeast Asia, as his successor Johnson did? We can never answer these or similar questions. But in rereading Kennedy's inaugural address, we can catch a glimpse of past hopes and an idealism that continues to evoke the best in us even now.

Sincerely,

Julia

Julia Hargrove

John F. Kennedy's Inaugural Address & Paraphrase

1) Vice President Johnson, Mr. Speaker, Mr. Chief Justice, President Eisenhower, Vice President Nixon, President Truman, Reverend Clergy, Fellow Citizens:

2) We observe today not a victory of party but a celebration of freedom—symbolizing an end as well as a beginning—signifying renewal as well as change. For I have sworn before you and Almighty God the same solemn oath our forebearers prescribed nearly a century and three-quarters ago.

3) The world is very different now. For man holds in his mortal hands the power to abolish all forms of human poverty and all forms of human life. And yet the same revolutionary beliefs for which our forebearers fought are still at issue around the globe—belief that the rights of man come not from the generosity of the state but from the hand of God.

1) Vice President Johnson, Mr. Speaker of the House, Mr. Chief Justice of the Supreme Court, Vice President Nixon, Reverend Clergy, Fellow Citizens:

2) What we see today is a celebration of freedom, not a victory of one political party over another. It is a symbol of renewal and change. I have sworn to you and God the same pledge our ancestors wrote in the Constitution nearly 175 years ago.

3) The world is different than it was 175 years ago. We have the ability to end both human poverty and all human life. Yet the same ideals of the American Revolution are still alive around the world. That idea is that God gives human rights to us, not any government.

John F. Kennedy's Inaugural Address & Paraphrase

4) We dare not forget today that we are the heirs of that first revolution. Let the word go forth from this time and place, to friend and foe alike, that the torch has been passed to a new generation of Americans—born in this century, tempered by war, disciplined by a hard and bitter peace, proud of our ancient heritage—and unwilling to witness or permit the slow undoing of those human rights to which this nation has always been committed and to which we are committed today at home and around the world.

5) Let every nation know, whether it wishes us well or ill, that we shall pay any price, bear any burden, meet any hardship, support any friend, oppose any foe to assure the survival and the success of liberty.

6) This much we pledge—and more.

7) To those old allies whose cultural and spiritual origins we share, we pledge the loyalty of faithful friends. United, there is little we cannot do in a host of co-operative ventures. Divided, there is little we can do—for we dare not meet a powerful challenge at odds and split asunder.

8) To those new states whom we welcome to the ranks of the free, we pledge our word that one form of colonial control shall not have passed away merely to be replaced by a far more iron tyranny. We shall not always expect to find them supporting our view. But we shall always hope to find them strongly supporting their own freedom—and to remember that, in the past, those who foolishly sought power by riding the back of the tiger ended up inside.

4) We should not forget that we inherited the ideas of the Revolution. Tell everyone, both our friends and enemies, starting here and now, that the power to govern has been passed to a new generation of Americans. These people were strengthened by World War II, taught self-discipline by the Cold War and made proud of their history of democracy. We will not watch or allow human rights to be taken away. We are now and always have been committed to human rights at home and around the world.

5) Let every nation know, whether it wishes us good luck or bad luck, that we will do anything to make sure liberty lives and succeeds.

6) We promise we will do this and more.

7) We will be loyal and faithful to our old allies who share our culture and religion. If we work together, there isn't anything we can't do. If we are divided, we can't do much at all. We must be united to meet the challenge of communism.

8) We welcome many new countries that have just gotten their independence. We promise them that their independence won't be taken away by a dictatorship. We don't expect them to always agree with us, but we do expect them to defend their own independence. Remember that people who tried to get power by riding the back of a tiger were eaten by the tiger.

John F. Kennedy's Inaugural Address & Paraphrase

9) To those people in the huts and villages of half the globe struggling to break the bonds of mass misery, we pledge our best efforts to help them help themselves, for whatever period is required—not because we seek their votes, but because it is right. If a free society cannot help the many who are poor, it cannot save the few who are rich.

10) To our sister republics south of our border, we offer a special pledge—to convert our good words into good deeds—in a new alliance for progress—to assist free men and free governments in casting off the chains of poverty. But this peaceful revolution of hope cannot become the prey of hostile powers. Let all our neighbors know that we shall join with them to oppose aggression or subversion anywhere in the Americas. And let every other power know that this hemisphere intends to remain the master of its own house.

11) To that world assembly of sovereign states, the United Nations, our last best hope in an age where the instruments of war have far outpaced the instruments of peace, we renew our pledge of support—to prevent it from becoming merely a forum for invective—to strengthen its shield of the new and the weak—and to enlarge the area in which its writ may run.

9) We promise the poor people in Africa, Asia and Latin America that we will help them help themselves for as long as they need us. We don't do this so they will vote on our side in the United Nations. We do it because it is the right thing to do. If we can't help the poor, we can't save the rich.

10) We promise the Latin American nations that we will change our good words into good deeds. We will create an alliance for progress to help them end poverty in their countries. But we cannot let this plan be destroyed by the Communists. We will join the Latin American countries to stop the invasion or internal overthrow of governments anywhere in our hemisphere. We will continue to be our own rulers.

11) The United Nations is the last, best hope for peace in a world which has the atomic bomb. We will support the U.N. We don't want it to become a place where nations only insult one another. We want it to defend the weak and newly independent countries and to make its power felt all over the world.

John F. Kennedy's Inaugural Address & Paraphrase

12) Finally, to those nations who would make themselves our adversary, we offer not a pledge but a request: that both sides begin anew the quest for peace, before the dark powers of destruction unleashed by science engulf humanity in planned or accidental self-destruction.

13) We dare not tempt them with weakness. For only when our arms are sufficient beyond doubt can we be certain beyond doubt that they will never be employed.

14) But neither can two great and powerful groups of nations take comfort from our present course—both sides overburdened by the cost of modern weapons, both rightly alarmed by the steady spread of the deadly atom, yet both racing to alter that uncertain balance of terror that stays the hand of mankind's final war.

15) So let us begin anew—remembering on both sides that civility is not a sign of weakness, and sincerity is always subject to proof. Let us never negotiate out of fear, but let us never fear to negotiate.

16) Let both sides explore what problems unite us instead of belaboring those problems which divide us.

17) Let both sides, for the first time, formulate serious and precise proposals for the inspection and control of arms—and bring the absolute power to destroy other nations under the absolute control of all nations.

12) We ask the countries that want to be our enemies to try again to create peace. We must do this before we accidentally or purposefully kill all humans with atomic bombs.

13) We must not cause our enemies to attack us because they think we are weak. We can only be safe when we have so many weapons that no country dares to attack us.

14) However, the U.S. and the Soviet Union can't be happy with the way things are going now. We are both paying too much for weapons, are frightened by the quickness of the spread of atomic weapons and are trying to stop the war that could kill us all.

15) Let's start over again. Being polite to each other is not a sign of weakness, but sincerity must be tested. We shouldn't make treaties because we are afraid of each other, but we shouldn't be afraid to make peace.

16) The U.S. and the Soviet Union should look at the problems we both have instead of going over the problems which make us enemies.

17) The U.S. and the Soviet Union should work seriously on plans to control weapons. All nations together should control the weapons that could destroy us all.

John F. Kennedy's Inaugural Address & Paraphrase

18) Let both sides seek to invoke the wonders of science instead of its terrors. Together let us explore the stars, conquer the deserts, eradicate disease, tap the ocean depths and encourage the arts and commerce.

19) Let both sides unite to heed in all corners of the earth the command of Isaiah—to "undo the heavy burdens . . . (and) let the oppressed go free."

20) And if a beachhead of co-operation may push back the jungle of suspicion, let both sides join in creating a new endeavor, not a new balance of power, but a new world of law, where the strong are just and the weak secure and the peace preserved.

21) All this will not be finished in the first one hundred days. Nor will it be finished in the first one thousand days, nor in the life of this administration, nor even perhaps in our lifetime on this planet. But let us begin.

22) In your hands, my fellow citizens, more than mine, will rest the final success or failure of our course. Since this country was founded, each generation of Americans has been summoned to give testimony to its national loyalty. The graves of young Americans who answered the call to service surround the globe.

23) Now the trumpet summons us again—not as a call to bear arms, though arms we need—not as a call to battle, though embattled we are—but a call to bear the burden of a long twilight struggle, year in and year out, "rejoicing in hope, patience in tribulation"—a struggle against the common enemies of man: tyranny, poverty, disease and war itself.

18) The U.S. and the Soviet Union should work to use science for good instead of for destruction. We should develop space travel, conquer the deserts, explore the resources of the ocean and help the arts and trade.

19) Both sides should do what Isaiah says. We should take away heavy burdens and let those who are slaves be free.

20) If cooperation can end suspicion, both sides should begin again. We should not create a new balance of power, we should make a world of laws. The strong nations should follow the laws so the weak nations enjoy safety and peace.

21) We won't be able to reach these goals in one hundred days or one thousand days or during my presidency or even in our lifetime. But we should begin.

22) The success of these goals is up to you more than it is up to me. Since the beginning of our country, each generation has been asked to prove its loyalty to the U.S. The graves of young Americans who served their country are found around the world.

23) Now we are asked again to serve our country. We won't fight with weapons; we fight a Cold War that will continue for many years. We must be hopeful but also patient when things go wrong. We will fight the common enemies of all people: dictators, poverty, diseases and war.

John F. Kennedy's Inaugural Address & Paraphrase

24) Can we forge against these enemies a grand and global alliance, North and South, East and West, that can assure a more fruitful life for all mankind? Will you join in that historic effort?

25) In the long history of the world, only a few generations have been granted the role of defending freedom in its hour of maximum danger. I do not shrink from this responsibility—I welcome it. I do not believe that any of us would exchange places with any other people or any other generation. The energy, the faith, the devotion which we bring to this endeavor will light our country and all who serve it—and the glow from that fire can truly light the world.

24) If we can fight these enemies by uniting the whole world, we can make a better life for all people. Will you join in trying to do this?

25) Only a few generations have had to defend freedom when it was most in danger. I welcome this responsibility. I don't think any of us would want to trade places with other generations. If we behave with energy, faith and loyalty, we will inspire our country and our people. That inspiration will be a fire that will light up the world.

"...ask not what your country can do for you...ask what you can do for your country."

26) And so, my fellow Americans, ask not what your country can do for you—ask what you can do for your country.

27) My fellow citizens of the world: ask not what America will do for you, but what together we can do for the freedom of man.

28) Finally, whether you are citizens of America or citizens of the world, ask of us here the same high standards of strength and sacrifice which we ask of you. With a good conscience our only sure reward, with history the final judge of our deeds, let us go forth to lead the land we love, asking His blessing and His help, but knowing that here on earth God's work must truly be our own.

26) Americans, don't ask what your country can do for you; ask what you can do for your country.

27) People of the world, don't ask what the U.S. can give you; ask what we can do together to keep men free.

28) Finally, citizens of America or of the world, ask our government to have the same high standards of strength and sacrifice that we ask of you. We will lead the land we love knowing that a good conscience and the judgment of history are our only rewards. We ask for God's blessing, but we know that we are the ones who must do God's work on Earth.

Name _____

Building a Time Line

On pages 12 and 13 are two time lines—one about Cuba and one about Berlin. Combine these two sets of events into a single time line of Kennedy's presidency from January 1961 through November 1963. As you weave the events, be sure to keep them in the correct time order.

January 20, 1961–Kennedy was sworn in as President of the United States.

January 1962

January 1963

November 22, 1963–President Kennedy was assassinated.

Cuba and the Cold War Time Line

Dec. 1898–U.S. gains possession of Cuba after having won the Spanish-American War and taking Cuba from Spain.

1902–U.S. grants Cuba its independence (May 20, 1902), but adds Platt Amendment which gives the U.S. the power to interfere in Cuban affairs.

1906–U.S. takes military control of Cuba for 13 days in October at the request of the Cuban president.

1912–U.S. Marines land in Cuba to protect U.S. interests.

1930s–U.S. begins Good Neighbor policy under President Franklin D. Roosevelt.

1933–Fulgencio Batista begins domination of Cuba either as president or main policy maker. His presidency is actually a cruel dictatorship.

1956–Fidel Castro lands in Oriente Province with a band of guerilla soldiers.

1958–Castro wins with revolution against Batista.

Jan. 1, 1959–Castro enters Havana in triumph and declares himself a dictator.

1960–Castro makes it clear that he is a Communist and receives a visit from the Soviet Union's deputy premier.

Jan. 3, 1961–U.S. breaks off diplomatic relations with Cuba.

Apr. 17, 1961–Cuban exiles invade Cuba at the Bay of Pigs. In spite of training by the CIA and U.S. military support. The invasion is crushed in a few days.

Feb. 3, 1962–President Kennedy orders a complete end to trade with Cuba.

Apr. 8, 1962–Castro says Bay of Pigs prisoners are convicted of treason and demands $62 million ransom for the release of 1179 men.

July-Aug. 1962–Soviets land missiles, fighter planes and technicians in Cuba.

Oct. 14, 1962–U.S. has evidence from *U-2* spy planes that there are missiles in Cuba.

Oct. 23, 1962–U.S. and the Organization of American States together announce an embargo of Cuba. They will use ships to keep out Soviet ships carrying missiles.

Oct. 27, 1962–Soviet Premier Khrushchev offers to withdraw missiles from Cuba.

Nov. 2, 1962–Kennedy says missiles in Cuba are being removed by U.S.S.R.

Nov. 20, 1962–Kennedy announces end of naval blockade of Cuba.

Dec. 3, 1962–Cuba begins letting Bay of Pigs prisoners go in return for $50 million in food and medicine from a committee of private U.S. citizens.

Name _____

Berlin and the Cold War Time Line

May 7-8, 1945–Work War II ended in Europe. Berlin and Germany jointly occupied by the Allies: U.S., Britain, France and Soviet Union. (Berlin was 110 miles inside the Soviet zone of Germany.)

1945-1948–Cold War developed between the U.S.S.R. and the other three former Allies.

Mar. 1948–U.S., Britain and France announced they would unite their zones to create the Federal Republic of Germany (West Germany). The Soviet Union did not give up its zone but created the Democratic Republic of Germany (East Germany) instead.

June 24, 1948–Soviet Union set up a blockade around the U.S., British and French zones in Berlin so that no food, fuel, medicine, etc., could get into or out of the city.

1948-1949–For 321 days, the U.S. and British air forces flew everything needed by the city into Berlin.

Apr. 4, 1949–Western European nations, the U.S. and Canada established the North Atlantic Treaty Organization promising to defend one another if attacked by the U.S.S.R.

May 1949–Stalin ended the blockade of the Western zones in Berlin. Minor harassment and closures continued through succeeding years, however.

1954–West Germany joined the North Atlantic Treaty Organization.

Nov. 27, 1958–Khrushchev demanded that the Allies be out of Berlin in six months.

May-June 1959–The six-month deadline passed, and Khrushchev did nothing. Crisis faded away.

Aug. 12-13, 1961–East Germany built a wall to cut off East Berlin from West Berlin. Citizens of East Germany could no longer escape into free West Berlin as easily.

Aug. 1961–President Kennedy called up U.S. reserve troops. The possibility of war between the U.S. and the Soviet Union was high.

Sept.-Dec. 1961–The threat of war lessened, and the U.S. accepted the existence of the wall.

1989–The Berlin Wall was torn down by East and West Germans.

Oct. 2, 1990–East and West Germany were united into one country. Berlin was again the capital of Germany.

Feb. 1, 1992–Presidents Bush and Yeltsin said the Cold War was officially over.

Name _____

Berlin and the Cold War Writing Exercise Outlining

Below is an outline that divides the events of the Berlin time line on the previous page into five main topics. Under the five main headings are several subtopics. You are to use the time line to find the events that belong in the subtopics. All of the subtopics will be about the same event as the main heading above them. One example is done for you.

I. Cold War Beginnings 1945-48

   A. The U.S., Britain and France united their zones into the Federal Republic of Germany (West Germany).

   B. The Soviet Union refused to allow East Germany to join West Germany and created the Democratic Republic of Germany (East Germany).

II. The Berlin Blockade 1948-49

   A.

   B.

   C.

III. Khrushchev and Berlin 1958

   A.

   B.

IV. The Berlin Wall 1961-1989

   A.

   B.

   C.

   D.

V. Berlin Wall, Germany and End of Cold War 1989-1992

   A.

   B.

14

Name _____

Berlin and the Cold War
Writing Exercise   Writing a Paragraph

Below is a question about the Cold War events in Berlin. Write your answer in complete sentences in the space provided. Use specific events from the time line to support your explanation.

Which of the five main events in Berlin do you think was most dangerous and most likely to have caused a war between the United States and the Soviet Union? Explain your answer.

15

TLC10222 Copyright © Teaching & Learning Company, Carthage, IL 62321-0010

Biography of John F. Kennedy

John F. Kennedy came from a long line of Irish politicians. His grandfather Patrick J. Kennedy served in the Massachusetts House of Representatives, the state Senate and in the government of Boston. His grandfather on his mother's side, John F. Fitzgerald, was elected to the Massachusetts Senate, the U.S. House of Representatives and the post of mayor of Boston. Joseph P. Kennedy, John's father, held two government positions under Franklin D. Roosevelt including that of ambassador to Britain. John and his brothers Robert and Edward all followed the family's political tradition, too.

John Fitzgerald Kennedy was born in Massachusetts on May 29, 1917. He had a back problem and suffered many childhood illnesses, but he was physically active in spite of those problems. Illness postponed his graduation from college, but he got his diploma from Harvard in 1940.

In 1941, the United States declared war on Japan, Germany and Italy; and Kennedy joined the navy although his back still bothered him. He became a war hero in August 1943 when a Japanese destroyer rammed his PT boat, and Kennedy saved the life of one of his men by pulling the sailor by his life jacket strap held in Kennedy's teeth. For this brave act, Admiral Halsey awarded Kennedy the Navy and Marine Corps medal.

Biography of John F. Kennedy

Following the war, Kennedy worked briefly as a journalist and then ran for the House of Representatives in 1946. He served in the House from 1947-53 and in the U.S. Senate from 1953-1961. He wanted to be nominated as the democratic vice presidential candidate in 1956, but he lost to another senator.

Meanwhile in 1953, Kennedy married Jacqueline Bouvier. They had two children: Caroline, born in 1957; and John, Jr. born in 1960. Kennedy had back surgery in 1954 and nearly died from an infection that he caught after the surgery. During the time he spent getting well, he wrote *Profiles in Courage,* a book about U.S. senators who put their political careers in danger by doing what was right rather than what was popular. His book won the Pulitzer Prize for biography.

Kennedy gained the Democratic nomination for President in 1960. The campaign against Richard Nixon was highlighted by the four televised debates between the two candidates. Kennedy's Catholic religion was also an issue, but he won the election with **49.7%** of the vote against Nixon's **49.5%**.

Kennedy's administration began with the failed Bay of Pigs invasion in Cuba. He overcame this defeat to deal more successfully with crises over the Berlin Wall, Soviet missiles in Cuba and increasing involvement in the Vietnam conflict. His presidency ended on November 22, 1963, when Lee Harvey Oswald assassinated him as he and his wife rode through Dallas, Texas.

Questions

1. What influence do you think Kennedy's family had on his choice of career?
2. Describe how Kennedy's illnesses affected his childhood, young adulthood and early career as a senator.
3. Do you think that Kennedy's action in WWII was heroic? Explain.
4. Kennedy was elected to what three political offices?
5. What things do you think Kennedy might have done for his country if he had not been killed and had been elected to a second term as President?

Name _____

President Kennedy and the Cold War

Map Exercise

You have three maps: the Western Hemisphere, Europe and Asia. Follow the directions below in coloring, outlining and labeling your maps. On each map, make a key showing the colors you used and what they mean.

I. Map of Western Hemisphere
   A. Label each country on this map with its name.
   B. Cuba is the only Communist country in the Western Hemisphere. Pick a "hot" color for Cuba and color in the island.
   C. Canada and the United States are members of the North Atlantic Treaty Organization that was formed to protect Western Europe and North America from the Soviet Union. Use a second color to outline these two countries.
   D. All of the nations in the Western Hemisphere except Cuba and Canada were members of the Alliance for Progress that Kennedy proposed in his inaugural address. Choose a third color to outline the members of this alliance. Be aware that the United States will be outlined in two colors when you have finished.

II. Map of Europe
   A. This map shows Europe as it looked before the breakup of the Soviet Union, which is how it was when Kennedy was President. Label each country with its name.
   B. The Communist countries in Eastern Europe were the Soviet Union, East Germany, Poland, Hungary, Czechoslovakia, Yugoslavia, Albania, Bulgaria and Romania. Choose a color and outline these countries.
   C. The North Atlantic Treaty Organization (NATO) countries—in addition to Canada and the U.S.–were Belgium, Denmark, France, Britain, Iceland, Italy, Luxembourg, the Netherlands, Norway, Portugal, Greece, Turkey and West Germany. Outline these countries with the same color you used for NATO on the Western Hemisphere map.
   D. Berlin was a trouble spot several times during the Cold War. Draw a red star inside East Germany to represent Berlin and write the city's name beside it.

III. Map of Asia
   A. Label the following nations with their names: China, North and South Korea, North and South Vietnam, Laos, Cambodia and India.
   B. Mainland China, North Korea and North Vietnam were Communist nations in Asia. Choose one color for all three and outline them.
   C. Communists fought in Laos and Cambodia to take them over, also. Outline them with a second color.

18

TLC10222 Copyright © Teaching & Learning Company, Carthage, IL 62321-0010

Name _____

Map of Western Hemisphere

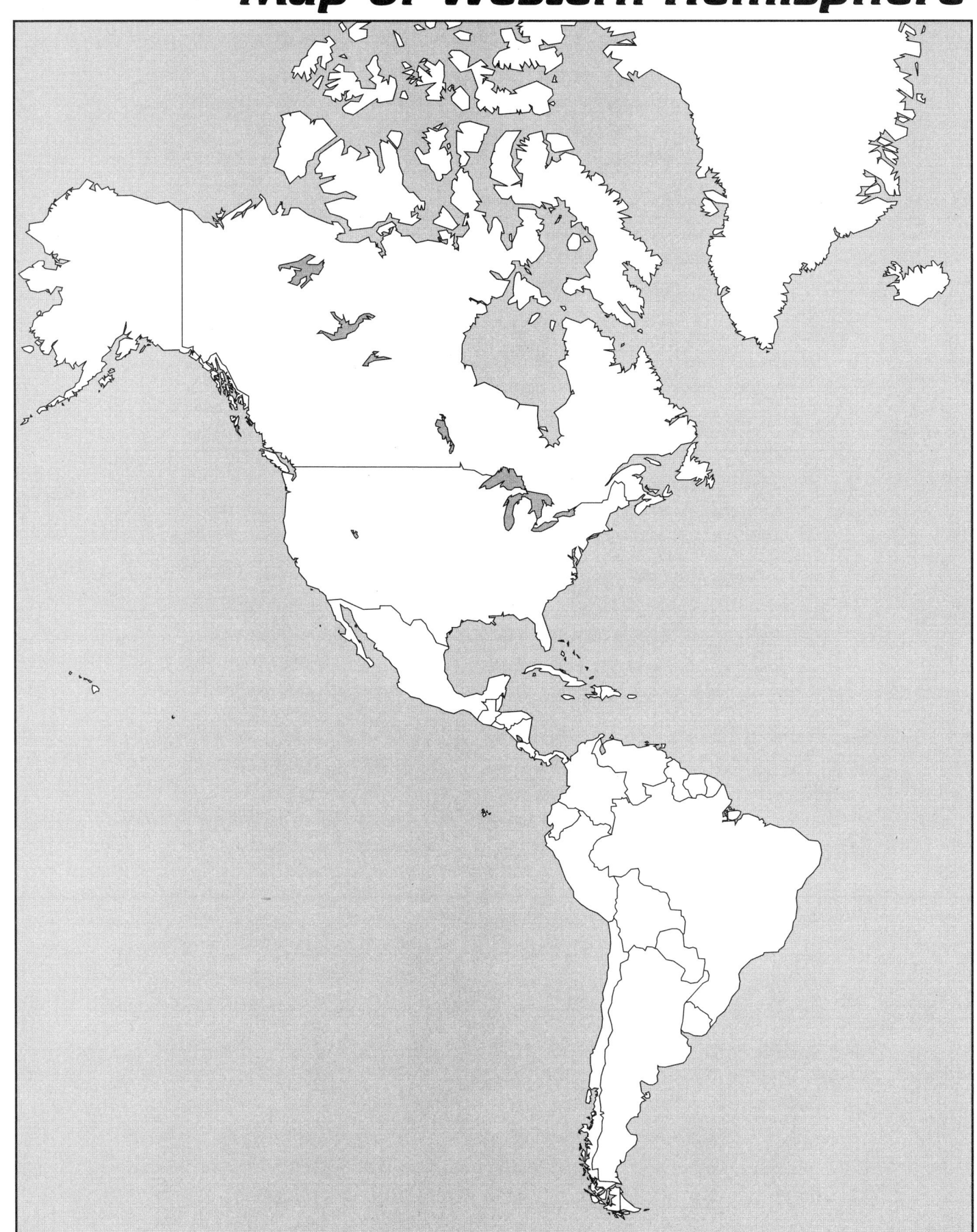

Name _____

Map of Europe

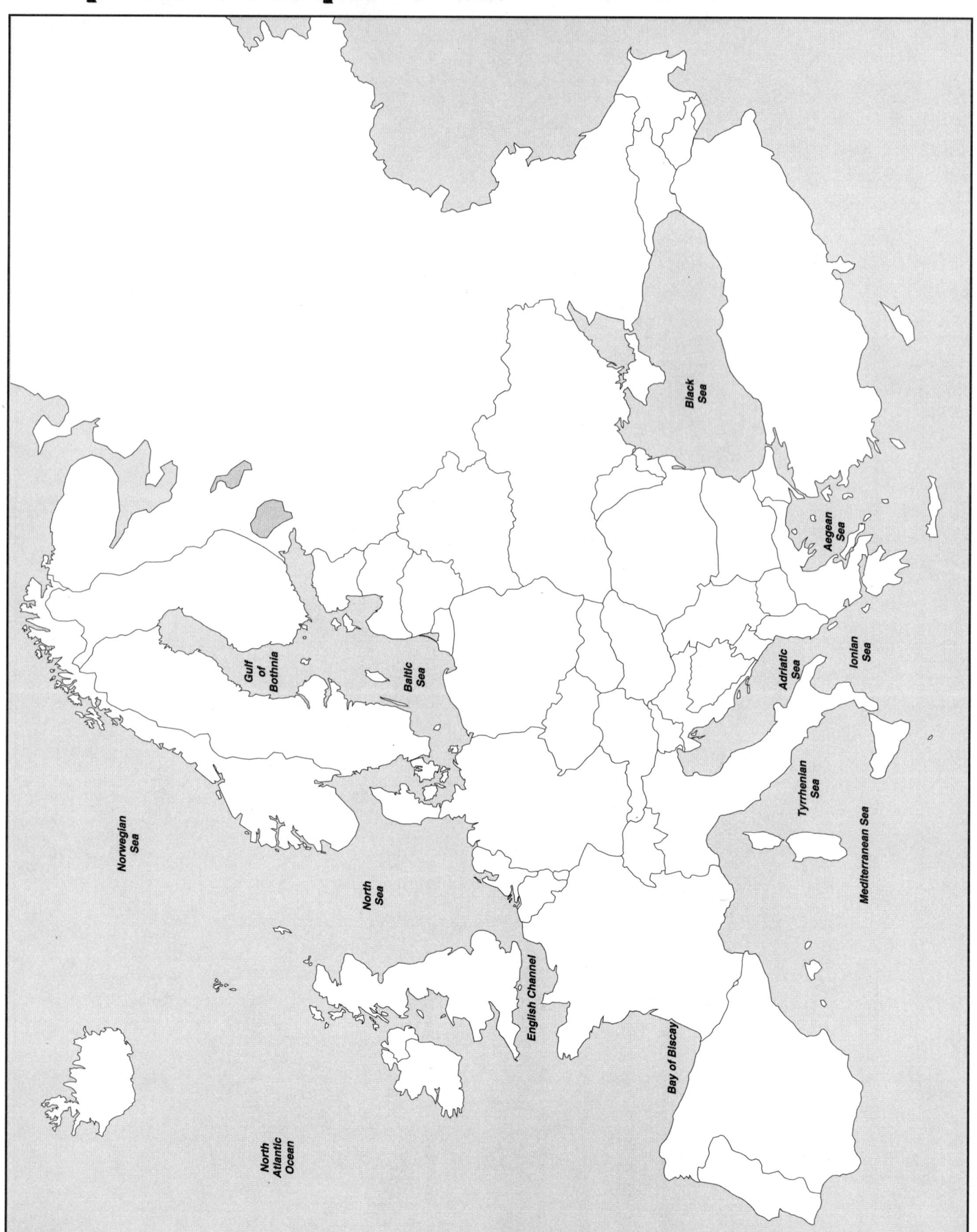

Name _____

Map of Asia

21

Latin America and the Alliance for Progress

To our sister republics south of our border, we offer a special pledge—to convert our good words into good deeds—in a new alliance for progress—to assist free men and free governments in casting off the chains of poverty.

John F. Kennedy's Inaugural Address

The United States' interest in the Latin American nations goes back to the 1810s and 1820s when those countries were winning their independence from Spain and Brazil. To protect that independence, President Monroe issued the Monroe Doctrine. The main idea was that the U.S. would prevent European countries from reconquering the newly independent nations.

However, in the following century, the United States proved a greater threat to the Latin American countries than any European nation. In 1836, the U.S. settlers in Texas won their independence from Mexico, taking that land away from Latin America. The U.S. declared war on Mexico in 1846 and took California, New Mexico, Arizona and parts of other states from that country. The U.S. fought the Spanish-American War in 1898 and gained Cuba and Puerto Rico. The U.S. granted Cuba its independence, but the Platte Amendment gave Americans the right to interfere in Cuban affairs. The U.S. took advantage of this power on several occasions.

The United States needed a canal across Central America so that U.S. fighting ships could travel more quickly from coast to coast. In November 1903, the U.S. supported a revolution in Panama against the government of Colombia. In return, Panama granted the U.S. a strip of land for a canal. The U.S. also interfered in the government finances of the Dominican Republic, Venezuela, Cuba, Honduras, Haiti and Nicaragua. Latin Americans deeply disliked the "Yankee Colossus," the U.S. "Bad Neighbor" to the north.

Latin America and the Alliance for Progress

President Hoover set the stage between 1928 and 1932 for what was to become Franklin D. Roosevelt's "Good Neighbor" policy. Hoover made a goodwill tour of Latin America and withdrew U.S. troops from Haiti and Nicaragua. Roosevelt proclaimed his "policy of the Good Neighbor" in his first inaugural address. The U.S. agreed not to interfere in Latin American affairs and proved its good intentions in Haiti, Cuba and Panama.

President Kennedy introduced his Alliance for Progress in his inaugural speech. Its purposes were to end poverty, reduce disease, improve the countries' economies and help more people learn to read. Kennedy hoped that improved living conditions would help fight the spread of Communism from Cuba to other Latin American nations. The United States and every Latin American country except Cuba signed a treaty at the conference in Punta del Este, Uruguay. Over the next 10 years, the U.S. was to give $20 billion in goods and services to Latin America. However, in the next decade, U.S. aid did not improve conditions. Unemployment, housing, the economic situation and the ability to read were either the same or worse than they had been before. The U.S. invasion of Cuba at the Bay of Pigs and intervention during the Cuban Missile Crisis showed the U.S. in the same old bad light. When President Nixon reduced aid to Latin America in 1972, the Alliance for Progress was as good as dead.

Questions

1. What did the U.S. do in 1823 to try to help the new Latin American countries?
2. Describe two situations in which the U.S. interfered in Latin American countries.
3. Which two Presidents began making the U.S. into a "Good Neighbor" instead of a bad one?
4. Describe in two sentences the purpose of the Alliance for Progress.
5. What is one of the reasons why the Alliance for Progress failed to help Latin Americans?

President Kennedy and the United Nations

To that world assembly of sovereign states, the United Nations, our last best hope in an age where the instruments of war have far outpaced the instruments of peace, we renew our pledge of support....

President Kennedy's Inaugural Address

The United Nations grew out of World War II and the failure of the earlier League of Nations. President Wilson of the United States proposed the idea of a union of nations as part of his Fourteen Points at the end of World War I. The Treaty of Versailles created the League, and many European nations joined it. Ironically, the United States, the country of the man who had proposed the League, refused to join. This was one of the serious weaknesses of the world organization. When the dictators of the fascist countries used aggression to conquer other nations in the 1930s, the League was either too weak or too frightened of causing a war to stop them.

At the end of World War II, the victorious Allies founded another world organization. Among the goals of the United Nations was preservation of peace and human rights. The U.N. has three branches of government: the Secretariat, the General Assembly and the Security Council. Every nation that is a member of the U.N. has an ambassador who is part of the General Assembly. The General Assembly is like the House of Representatives in the U.S. government. The Secretary General, who is like our President in his job, is elected by the members of the General Assembly. The branch that is most like the U.S. Senate is the Security Council. It is composed of 15 countries. Five were the original Allies in World War II and are permanent members: France, Britain, the U.S.S.R., the United States and China. (In the 1970s, Communist China replaced Chinese Taiwan in the U.N.) The other 10 nations on the Security Council have two-year terms in office and are chosen from the members of the General Assembly. The five permanent members have a veto power over actions proposed by members of the United Nations. This organization also works to help people of the world through its own agencies such as the World Health Organization and the United Nations Relief and Rehabilitation Administration.

President Kennedy and the United Nations

The U.N. has had a strong role in keeping peace in the world since its beginnings. It caused the Soviet Union to withdraw troops from Iran in 1946 and settled a dispute between the Jews and Arabs in Palestine in 1947. In 1950, the Security Council (with the Soviet Union absent) voted to send troops to South Korea to fight the invasion of the North Koreans. In 1961, Secretary Dag Hammarskjold died in a plane crash while on his way to try to settle a civil war in the Congo. Later, the rebellious province rejoined the rest of its country. Although the United Nations has had its failures, it continues to work to resolve disputes between nations.

Questions

1. What world organization tried to keep the peace between World War I and World War II?
2. What were the five most powerful nations on the Security Council when the U.N. was created?
3. Which of the three branches of the U.N. has the power to veto actions by other members?
4. What are two situations that the U.N. has resolved to keep peace in the world?
5. Make a drawing showing the three branches of the United Nations, their members and their powers.
6. Are you in favor of or against a world organization such as the United Nations? Explain your answer with at least three reasons.

Multiple Intelligence Activities

These activities are designed to appeal to one or more of the identified "intelligences" and relate directly or peripherally to John F. Kennedy's inaugural address.

Verbal/Linguistic Intelligence

1. Two students will be John Kennedy and Richard Nixon in the first televised presidential debate. They should pick two topics important in the early 1960s, write the main arguments of their debate and perform the debate in front of the class.

2. Students could memorize parts of Kennedy's inaugural address and deliver it in appropriate oratorical style to fellow students.

Visual/Spatial Intelligence

1. Design the television set for the Nixon-Kennedy debates. What should the background to the set and the speakers' stands look like? Where should the two debators and the moderator be placed on the set? What colors should be used to show the best contrast on black-and-white TV? How should the men dress so that they stand out clearly against the background of the set?

2. Jacqueline Kennedy impressed people with her sense of style and fashion. Women imitated her look from her dresses to her hairstyle and her pillbox hats. Her fashion sense was quite different from that of the previous First Lady, Mamie Eisenhower. Find pictures of what both women wore and make a collage contrasting the major features of their clothing. You could also design new clothing for each woman using her style.

3. One of Mrs. Kennedy's most notable achievements as First Lady was her redecoration of the White House in a style most like its original one.

    a. Find pictures of the redecorated rooms and the restored furniture and make a collage showing the new features.

    b. Find pictures of both the old décor under the Eisenhowers and the new decor of Mrs. Kennedy. Make a visual display and explain the main differences in the styles.

    c. Mrs. Kennedy made a tour of the redecorated White House for television. Make a slide show or videotape your own tour of the new rooms.

Music/Auditory Intelligence

1. Write songs imitating the new musical forms of the early 1960s. You might imitate Elvis Presley's style, folk songs, the rhythm of the Twist or protest songs like those of Bob Dylan. Sing and play your song(s) for the class.

2. Students research the bands, singers and songs of the 1960s for a report on how this music reflected the times. They might make an audiotape of the favorite music and narrate a history of the music styles and performers between songs.

Multiple Intelligence Activities

Mathematical Intelligence

1. Make a chart or bar graph showing the numbers of U.S. deaths in each of our country's wars. This chart or graph would include the American Revolution, the War of 1812, the Mexican-American War, the Spanish-American War, World War I, World War II, the Korean conflict, the Vietnam War and Desert Storm (the Persian Gulf War).

2. Research the U.S. space program from 1961 to 1969 (when the U.S. landed its first men on the moon).

   a. Compile and display statistics about the space program such as the cost of each mission, the distances each mission went, the length of time each mission was in space or the ages and years of experience of each astronaut.

   b. After doing research on the U.S. and Russian space programs, make a time line showing the rivalry and successes of each country. Your time line should cover the years from 1957 (when the U.S.S.R. put its first object into orbit around the Earth) to 1969 (the first manned U.S. moon landing).

Kinesthetic Intelligence

1. The Kennedy-Nixon debates were the first time two political opponents for the office of President appeared on national television to exchange their views and opinions. Many people feel the difference in "body language" between the debators was as significant an influence on the voting public as anything either of them had to say. View as much of the debates as you can obtain and describe or reenact the physical styles of the two participants.

2. The Kennedy family enjoyed playing touch football during family gatherings. Because of their enjoyment of sports, a physical fitness craze spread across the United States, including attempts by many people to hike 50 miles in 24 hours. Organize the students in a touch football game or design a series of exercises which students can do for a week or more in a physical fitness program.

Interpersonal Intelligence

1. Several students can play the roles of reporters after the Bay of Pigs invasion of Cuba or the end of the Cuban Missile Crisis. Write your questions in advance and be sure to make the questions difficult. Then role-play a press conference with reporters questioning President Kennedy.

2. President Kennedy became very angry when many steel companies raised their prices at the same time. He was especially angry because he had just persuaded laborers to accept a small pay raise instead of the larger one the workers wanted.

   a. Students can play the parts of President Kennedy and the owners of the steel mills as Kennedy bawls them out and makes them lower their prices.

   b. Teach students the rules of conflict resolution. Then have them role-play a confrontation in which Kennedy makes the workers and the steel mill owners compromise on wage increases for laborers.

Multiple Intelligence Activities

Intrapersonal Intelligence

1. Robert F. Kennedy was President Kennedy's brother, Attorney General and one of his closest advisors. They spoke with each other frequently during the Cuban Missile Crisis. Write an imaginary conversation between the two men discussing their thoughts and feelings about the burdens of power and their philosophies of life.

2. Pretend that you are one of the first people to join the Peace Corps. You are sent to a country you have never visited, and you have to adjust to a different culture and language. You are living with poor people because they are the ones who need your help. Research the living conditions in a country in Africa, Asia or Latin America during the 1960s. Then write several diary entries describing your efforts to adjust and the new friends you make there.

Multiple Intelligences

1. Reenact parts of the 1960 presidential campaign. Students can write and illustrate television ads; write campaign speeches on major issues; plan a campaign itinerary; role-play the democratic or republican national convention during which each candidate won his party's nomination; draw symbols for the campaign and write slogans; play inspiring music at the convention; design hats, banners, key chains and other favors to give to prospective voters; or make a videotaped biography of the candidate.

Internet Research Ideas

1. Students might research the biographies of famous people: Ho Chi Minh; Nikita Khrushchev; Dwight D. Eisenhower; Lyndon Johnson; Lee Harvey Oswald; Jack Ruby; Richard Nixon; Martin Luther King, Jr.; Fidel Castro; U.N. Secretary General Dag Hammarskjold; Jacqueline Bouvier Kennedy and Che Guevarra.

2. Research John F. Kennedy's assassination and funeral and the death of Lee Harvey Oswald, the whole four days.

3. Some research topics about popular music include: the payola scandal among disc jockies; the Beatles 1963 and 1964 and Shea Stadium in New York; folk music; the group of Peter, Paul and Mary; Joan Baez; the Kingston Trio and Elvis Presley's continuing career.

4. Find out about the 1963 assassination of Ngo Dinh Diem, President of South Vietnam, only three weeks before President Kennedy was killed.

5. Broadway musicals from the early 1960s that have become classics include: *How to Succeed in Business Without Really Trying; Camelot; Bye, Bye, Birdie; A Funny Thing Happened on the Way to the Forum; The Fantastics* and *The Sound of Music*. Find out more about these musicals, their stars and their authors. Perhaps you can play or sing some of their songs for your class.

6. Watch and write reviews on some of the movies from the early 1960s. *Ben Hur* is an example of a movie that won several Oscars.

7. There were many good TV shows in the 1960s including some that you can see today on cable channels. Research and watch: *21, Perry Mason, The Andy Griffith Show, The Defenders, Hazel, The Dick Van Dyke Show* or other shows.

8. Fidel Castro established the first Communist government in the Western Hemisphere. Find out about his revolution against the Cuban dictator, his victory and his turn to Communism once he was in power.

9. The U.S. involvement in Vietnam was a long, complex process. Starting with the defeat of the French in 1954, tell how the U.S. commitment to Vietnam grew until the U.S. was in a full-fledged war under President Johnson.

10. Military weapons developed after the invention of the atomic bomb were very different in use before the bomb. Find out about the planes, rifles, missiles, tanks, atomic-powered submarines, aircraft carriers, defoliants and other weapons.

11. For a larger picture of the Cold War, research the Hungarian revolt against Communism in 1956 or the one in Czechoslovakia in 1968. What did the people want, and what did the Soviets do about the revolts?

12. Learn about the efforts in Kennedy's administration to end nuclear testing in the atmosphere and to regulate the growth of nuclear weapons through international inspections. One place to start would be with the Strategic Arms Limitations talks.

Internet Research Ideas

13. Do more specific research on the Bay of Pigs invasion of Cuba, who planned it, why it was done and the results of the U.S. defeat there. G. Gordon Liddy and E. Howard Hunt, who were involved in planning the invasion, make another appearance in Richard Nixon's presidency.

14. The Cuban Missile Crisis has more exciting information than is found in the time line on Cuba in this book. To get a feeling for the tension over the missiles, you might watch *The Missiles of October*. Also research the events and the personalities involved: John and Robert Kennedy and Nikita Khrushchev.

15. Look into the construction of the Berlin Wall on August 12-13, 1961, and the crisis it caused. Even more fascinating are the stories of the people who tried to escape over the wall to freedom in West Berlin.

16. Learn more about the Alliance for Progress. Research a specific Latin American country to see what the money did there, or look up the program from the U.S. point of view.

17. Rachel Carson wrote *Silent Spring* that was a book about pesticides and how they were killing birds. Research Carson, read parts of her book and learn about the beginning of the environmental movement.

18. Guantanamo naval base in Cuba, which the U.S. has maintained in spite of Castro's Communist rule, has an interesting story. Learn about the base's history and what use the U.S. Navy makes of it now.

19. Skyjacking, the hijacking of airplanes while they were in flight, happened frequently. Many times people skyjacked a plane to get to Cuba. Investigate skyjacking and the strong laws that stopped it.

20. Baseball was filled with excitement during the early 1960s. Some topics you might research are Roger Maris and his 61 home runs that beat Babe Ruth's record of 60, Mickey Mantle's 60 home runs, the Yankees' winning streak in the World Series, manager Casey Stengel, catcher/coach Yogi Berra and the other teams and players.

21. Research the beginnings of the U.S. space programs in the 1950s and astronauts such as Alan Shepherd, Virgil "Gus" Grissom, John Glenn, M. Scott Carpenter and Walter N. Schirra. Investigate also the moon landing in July 1969.

22. Learn about the top boxers of this period: Floyd Patterson, Archie Moore, Sonny Liston, Casius Clay (later Muhammad Ali), Ingemar Johansson and others.

23. Find out about the athletes who competed in the winter Olympics in 1960 at Squaw Valley, California, and the summer Olympics that same year in Rome.

24. James R. "Jimmy" Hoffa had an interesting career as the long-time president of the Teamsters' Union. He was accused of misusing the Teamsters' funds, and later he was kidnapped and murdered. His body was never found.

Internet Research Ideas

25. Investigate professional basketball teams, players like Wilt Chamberlain or the highly talented African American players who were the Harlem Globe Trotters.

26. Study the election campaign of 1960, Nixon vs. Kennedy: the television debates, the issues of the election, the popular vote and the close results.

27. The United States and Canada built a Distant Early Warning system (DEW Line) to warn of atomic missiles coming from the Soviet Union over Siberia or the North Pole. Research the technology and construction of this system.

28. Investigate the Peace Corps, the countries and projects involved; what workers were expected to do and Sargent Shriver, director of Corps. You might also enjoy reading about Lillian Carter (mother of President Jimmy Carter) and her service in the Corps.

29. Investigate Jacqueline Kennedy's redecoration of the White House, getting back some of the original furniture and her tour of the White House on TV.

30. Telstar was the first communications satellite. It was engineered by AT&T and Bell Telephone Laboratories and changed television broadcasting forever.

31. The extension of civil rights to African Americans was important. Look up James H. Meredith and the integration of the University of Mississippi; Martin Luther King Jr.'s rally in Washington, D.C., and his "I Have a Dream" speech; the activities of the NAACP; Medgar Evers and other civil rights leaders.

32. Pop art was a new style of art in the 1960s. Find out about Andy Warhol and his fellow artists.

33. Research the Americans who have won the Nobel peace prize including Martin Luther King, Jr., in 1964; President Theodore Roosevelt; President Woodrow Wilson; Jane Addams; Ralph Bunche; Vice President Charles Dawes and Secretary of State Cordell Hull.

34. Learn about the history of the persecution of Catholics in the U.S.; Al Smith, the only Catholic to run for President before John Kennedy and how Kennedy handled the issue of his religion during the 1960 presidential campaign.

Answer Key

Building a Time Line, page 11

1961
Jan. 20–President Kennedy sworn in as President of the United States.

Apr. 17–Cuban exiles invaded Cuba at the Bay of Pigs.

Aug. 12-13–East Germany built a wall between East Berlin and West Berlin.

Aug.–President Kennedy called up U.S. reserve troops.

Sept.-Dec.–The threat of war lessened; U.S. accepted the wall.

1962
Feb. 3–President Kennedy orders a complete end to trade with Cuba.

Apr. 8–Castro says Bay of Pigs prisoners are convicted of treason; demanded ransom.

July-Aug.–Soviets land missiles, fighter planes and technicians in Cuba.

Oct. 14–U.S. has evidence from *U-2* spy planes that there are missiles in Cuba.

Oct. 23–U.S. and the Organization of American States together announce an embargo of Cuba.

Oct. 27–Soviet Premier Khrushchev offers to withdraw missiles from Cuba.

Nov. 2–Kennedy says missiles in Cuba are being removed by U.S.S.R.

Nov. 20–Kennedy announces end of naval blockade of Cuba.

Dec. 3–Cuba begins letting Bay of Pigs prisoners go . . .

1963
Nov. 22–President Kennedy was assassinated.

Berlin and the Cold War Writing Exercise, page 14

I. Cold War Beginnings 1945-48
   A. The U.S., Britain and France united their zones into the Federal Republic of Germany (West Germany).
   B. The Soviet Union refused to allow East Germany to join West Germany and created the Democratic Republic of Germany (East Germany).

II. The Berlin Blockade 1948-49
   A. Soviet Union blockaded the U.S., British and French zones in Berlin.
   B. For 321 days, the U.S. and British air forces flew everything into Berlin.
   C. Stalin ended the blockade of the western zones in Berlin.

III. Khrushchev and Berlin 1958
   A. Khrushchev demanded that the Allies be out of Berlin in six months.
   B. Six-month deadline passed; Khrushchev did nothing. Crisis ended.

IV. The Berlin Wall 1961-1989
   A. East Germany built a wall to cut off East Berlin from West Berlin.
   B. President Kennedy called up U.S. reserve troops. War highly possible.
   C. The threat of war lessened; the U.S. accepted the existence of the wall.
   D. East and West Germans tore down the Berlin Wall.

V. Berlin Wall, Germany and End of Cold War 1989-1992
   A. East and West Germany were united. Berlin was the capital again.
   B. Bush and Yeltsin officially declared the end of the Cold War.

Biography of John F. Kennedy, page 17

1. Kennedy might have been inspired to go into politics by his family's tradition of political service.
2. Kennedy was very ill in his childhood, but that didn't stop him from being active. His illness as a young adult kept him from graduating from college with his age mates. When he was a senator, he was ill and was not able to perform the duties of his office.
3. Answers will vary. They probably will think he was heroic because he saved a person's life.
4. Kennedy was elected to the House, the Senate and the presidency.
5. Answers will vary according to their age and knowledge.

Latin America and the Alliance for Progress, page 23

1. The U.S. proclaimed the Monroe Doctrine that told the European nations that the Western Hemisphere was not open for colonization any longer.
2. The U.S. took Texas away from Mexico, took California and the Southwest away from Mexico, took Cuba from Spain, helped the Panamanians revolt against Colombia in order to get the land for a canal and interfered in the finances or governments (usually with troops) of the Dominican Republic, Venezuela, Cuba, Honduras, Haiti and Nicaragua.
3. Herbert Hoover and Franklin D. Roosevelt started working on the Good Neighbor policy.
4. Kennedy hoped to end poverty, reduce disease, improve the countries' economies and help people learn to read. He also hoped that these improvements would help keep the Communists out of those countries.
5. The money spent did not improve conditions in Latin America. The U.S. made itself a bad neighbor with the Bay of Pigs invasion. And eventually the budget for the Alliance was cut.

President Kennedy and the United Nations, page 25

1. The League of Nations tried to keep the peace between World Wars I and II.
2. The five powerful nations on the Security Council were the U.S., Britain, France, China and the Soviet Union.
3. The Security Council has the veto power.
4. The U.N. got Soviet troops out of Iran, settled a dispute between Arabs and Jews in Palestine, fought the North Korean troops in the Korean War and helped settle the revolt of the Katanga province in the Congo.
5. General Assembly
   a. Like the U.S. House of Reps.
   b. Elects the Sec. General of U.N.
   c. Includes all member nations.
   d. Chooses 10 members of Sec. Council.
   Security Council
   a. Like the U.S. Senate.
   b. Made up of 15 members.
   c. Five members have veto power.
   Secretariat
   a. Sec. General is like the U.S. President.
   b. Secretariat is like the U.S. executive branch; it carries out the orders of other two branches.
6. Answers will vary.